BEAUTIFUL
ANGELS
COLORING BOOK

MARJORIE SARNAT

DOVER PUBLICATIONS, INC.
MINEOLA, NEW YORK

An angel's pure beauty is undeniable. On each page of this inspiring coloring book you'll find one or perhaps two or three of these elegant beings in a tranquil scene—amidst the clouds, in the heavens, playing melodies, and even befriending animals. With 31 illustrations in all, this book will provide colorists many opportunities to hone their skills. Plus, the pages are perforated and un-backed to make removing and displaying your finished artwork easy.

Copyright

Copyright © 2018 by Marjorie Sarnat
All rights reserved.

Bibliographical Note

Beautiful Angels Coloring Book is a new work,
first published by Dover Publications, Inc., in 2018.

International Standard Book Number

ISBN-13: 978-0-486-81857-3
ISBN-10: 0-486-81857-8

Manufactured in the United States by LSC Communications
81857805   2019
www.doverpublications.com

GUARDIAN ANGEL OF CATS

GUARDIAN ANGEL OF DOGS

SPRING

SUMMER

AUTUMN